Jonathan Edwards

Colonial Religious Leader

Norma Jean Lutz

Arthur M. Schlesinger, jr.
Senior Consulting Editor

Chelsea House Publishers

Philadelphia

Produced by Pre-Press Company, Inc., East Bridgewater, MA 02333

CHELSEA HOUSE PUBLISHERS
Editor in Chief Stephen Reginald
Production Manager Pamela Loos
Art Director Sara Davis
Director of Photography Judy L. Hasday
Managing Editor James D. Gallagher
Senior Production Editor J. Christopher Higgins

Staff for *JONATHAN EDWARDS*
Project Editor Anne Hill
Associate Art Director Takeshi Takahashi
Series Design Keith Trego

The Chelsea House World Wide Web address is http://www.chelseahouse.com

First Printing
1 3 5 7 9 8 6 4 2

Library of Congress Cataloging-in-Publication Data

Lutz, Norma Jean.
   Jonathan Edwards/Norma Jean Lutz.
      p. cm. — (Colonial Leaders)
   Includes bibliographical references (p.) and index.
   ISBN 0-7910-5961-8 (HC); 0-7910-6118 (PB)
      1. Edwards, Jonathan, 1703–1758—Juvenile literature. 2. Congregational
   churches—United States—Clergy—Biography—Juvenile literature. [1. Edwards,
   Jonathan, 1703–1758. 2. Clergy.] I. Title. II. Series.

BX7260.E3 L88 2000
285.8'092—dc21
[B]   00038400

Publisher's Note: In Colonial and Revolutionary War America, there were no standard rules for spelling, punctuation, capitalization, or grammar. Some of the quotations that appear in the Colonial Leaders and Revolutionary War Leaders series come from original documents and letters written during this time in history. Original quotations reflect writing inconsistencies of the period.

Jonathan Edwards

Colonial Religious Leader

Colonial Leaders

Lord Baltimore
English Politician and Colonist

Benjamin Banneker
American Mathematician and Astronomer

Sir William Berkeley
Governor of Virginia

William Bradford
Governor of Plymouth Colony

Jonathan Edwards
Colonial Religious Leader

Benjamin Franklin
American Statesman, Scientist, and Writer

Anne Hutchinson
Religious Leader

Cotton Mather
Author, Clergyman, and Scholar

Increase Mather
Clergyman and Scholar

James Oglethorpe
Humanitarian and Soldier

William Penn
Founder of Democracy

Sir Walter Raleigh
English Explorer and Author

Caesar Rodney
American Patriot

John Smith
English Explorer and Colonist

Miles Standish
Plymouth Colony Leader

Peter Stuyvesant
Dutch Military Leader

George Whitefield
Clergyman and Scholar

Roger Williams
Founder of Rhode Island

John Winthrop
Politician and Statesman

John Peter Zenger
Free Press Advocate

Revolutionary War Leaders

John Adams
Second U.S. President

Ethan Allen
Revolutionary Hero

Benedict Arnold
Traitor to the Cause

King George III
English Monarch

Nathanael Greene
Military Leader

Nathan Hale
Revolutionary Hero

Alexander Hamilton
First U.S. Secretary of the Treasury

John Hancock
President of the Continental Congress

Patrick Henry
American Statesman and Speaker

John Jay
First Chief Justice of the Supreme Court

Thomas Jefferson
Author of the Declaration of Independence

John Paul Jones
Father of the U.S. Navy

Lafayette
French Freedom Fighter

James Madison
Father of the Constitution

Francis Marion
The Swamp Fox

James Monroe
American Statesman

Thomas Paine
Political Writer

Paul Revere
American Patriot

Betsy Ross
American Patriot

George Washington
First U.S. President

Famous Figures of the Civil War Era

Jefferson Davis
Confederate President

Frederick Douglass
Abolitionist and Author

Ulysses S. Grant
Military Leader and President

Stonewall Jackson
Confederate General

Robert E. Lee
Confederate General

Abraham Lincoln
Civil War President

William Sherman
Union General

Harriet Beecher Stowe
Author of Uncle Tom's Cabin

Sojourner Truth
Abolitionist, Suffragist, and Preacher

Harriet Tubman
Leader of the Underground Railroad

Contents

Much of Jonathan Edwards's boyhood was spent in the woods observing the natural world and talking to God. Spiders making their webs particularly fascinated him. Edwards believed that God's presence could be directly experienced in the wonders of nature.

1

An Observant Child

The congregation in East Windsor, Connecticut, erected the finest house in town for their new minister, Timothy Edwards. Although most other houses in town were made of logs, this home was built of hewn lumber. The new **parsonage** was larger as well, with a second story overhanging the first in the common New England style. But as large as it was, the house would gain many assorted lean-tos, or additions, as children came along.

A single chimney separated the kitchen-living room and the parlor on the first floor. An eight-or nine-foot projection at the middle front of the house created a **vestibule.**

The young preacher had graduated from Harvard in November 1694 and four months later married Esther Stoddard. Eight days after the wedding, the couple traveled to East Windsor and moved into the new parsonage. Timothy Edwards became the town's first pastor, a position he would hold until his death.

Nine years and four daughters later, Timothy and Esther had a son whom they named Jonathan. Following his birth on October 5, 1703, the Edwardses would have six more daughters, with Jonathan being their only son.

Nearly every family in East Windsor farmed, including the minister. Reverend Timothy Edwards spent part of his time with work such as spring plowing and tanning hides for leather. The rest of his time was spent reading his Bible and writing sermons. Out on the frontier, the minister was not a person set apart from daily tasks as happened in larger cities such as Boston.

Members of the congregation cut wood for the preacher and brought him sugar, spices, and mutton to pay his "rate"–his pay for being the minister and for teaching their children. These payments were recorded in his rate book.

The Edwardses owned a large farm. There were fields to fertilize, crops to harvest, stock to care for, and dozens of other related chores. Some of this work was distasteful for Timothy Edwards, who had been reared in the city. Jonathan, however, came by farming more naturally.

Jonathan grew up in an area surrounded by meadows, forests, a river, many animals, and the neighborly spirit of a small village. Near the East Windsor meetinghouse stood a small fort (or palisade). For the previous generation, this was where the townspeople would gather in case of an Indian attack.

During Jonathan's boyhood, there were only about 100 families in East Windsor. Each house was built on its own acreage, which meant that the town was spread out over a wide area. This spaciousness must have allowed many play areas for the children of East Windsor.

The Edwardses' closest neighbors were the Stoughtons. Captain Thomas Stoughton had married Timothy Edwards's sister, Abigail. In this family were seven boys—three younger than Jonathan, three older, and one exactly his age. Even though he had no brothers with whom he could play, Jonathan was well supplied with companionship from the many cousins next door.

Across the Connecticut River lay the more populated settlement of Windsor, which had a meetinghouse larger than the one in East Windsor. Because taking a canoe across the river was a dangerous undertaking, the people of East Windsor were thankful to have their own meetinghouse and their own pastor.

The village school was in the parlor of the parsonage. On three sides of the room, benches were nailed to the wall. Here on these uncomfortable wooden benches, Jonathan, his sisters, his cousins, and other village children were taught by Reverend Timothy Edwards.

School in Jonathan's day was very rigorous. The students were expected to learn Latin, Greek, and Hebrew, and to recite lessons in front of the class. As a young boy, Jonathan attended the local village school.

School was rigorous. The children were taught Latin, Greek, and Hebrew. Their teacher required letter-perfect memorization. The attention paid to detail is revealed in a letter from Reverend Edwards while he was away from home. Writing to his wife, he directed her as to the children's schooling:

> I desire thee to take care that Jonathan dont loose what he hath Learned but that as he hath got the accidence, & above two sides of *propria Quae moribus* by heart so that he keep what he hath got, I would therefore have him Say pretty often to the girls; I would also have the Girls keep what they have Learnt of the Grammar, & get by heart as far as Jonathan had Learnt: he can help them to Read as far as he hath Learnt: and would have both him and them keep their writing, and therefore writer much oftener than they did when I was at home.

In back of the parsonage, the land sloped down to a brook, then up a hill to a densely wooded area. Here Jonathan would spend long hours alone talking to God and studying the many facets of the wonders of nature. From very early on, he was deeply religious and very concerned about his relationship with God.

As an adult he remembered back to a time of **"awakening"** in his father's church after which he was "affected for many months, and concerned about the things of religion." He also remembered going into the woods alone to pray five times a day. He and his schoolmates built a lean-to in the swamp where they all prayed together.

By spending time in the woods, Jonathan developed a keen sense of observation. Spiders and their webs fascinated him. At the age of 12, he began to define and classify the spiders he found. He wrote of the webs as "little shining webs and glistening strings of a great length and at such a height as that one would think that they were tacked to the sky by one end."

He especially wanted to solve the mystery of their webmaking. In his writings he explained the spider's navigation in the air, the character of the web, and his ideas of how the web is made.

Later he wrote equally well about his study of rainbows. He liked to practice making rainbows by spurting out a mouthful of water and watching

Jonathan enjoyed spending much of his free time experimenting in nature. One of his favorite experiments was making rainbows.

the sun turn the droplets to little rainbows. The fact that all this observing, writing, and classifying was completed with no training in science is remarkable. It has been said that had Jonathan Edwards not been so bent on **theology**, he might have become a scientist like Benjamin Franklin.

But the life of a scientist was not an option. Jonathan grew up in the parsonage. The few out-of-town visitors he met during those years were visiting clergymen. Conversations nearly always centered around religious matters. But even if there had not been these strong family ties to religion, chances are Jonathan would still have become a minister, simply because of the deep religious beliefs he had as a child.

He wrote of "conversing with Christ," and being "wrapt and swallowed up in God." Walking in his father's pasture, he began to sense the majesty of God and then saw God's hand in everything around him.

> God's excellency, his wisdom, his purity and love, seemed to appear in every thing; in the sun, moon and stars; in the clouds, and the blue sky; in the grass, flowers, trees; in the water, and all nature; which used greatly to fix my mind.

At age 13, his times of wandering through quiet woods and meadows came to an end. Jonathan's childhood days were over; in 1716 he was enrolled in the Collegiate School of Connecticut in New Haven (later known as Yale College).

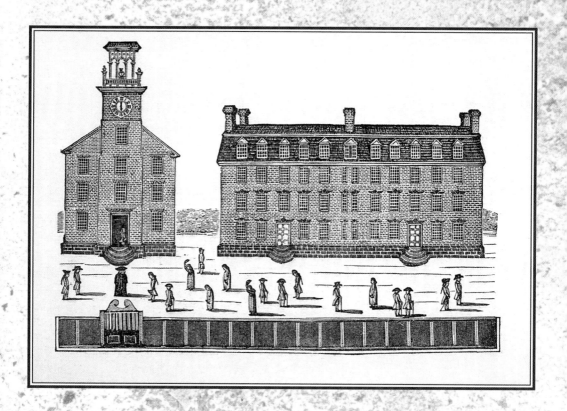

As a member of the first class to attend
Yale College, Jonathan took advantage of
the school's vast library to read and study
a variety of subjects.

The Years at Yale

Jonathan Edwards became one of a class of 10 boys at the Collegiate School in the fall of 1716. Founded only two years before Jonathan's birth, the college had already fallen into disrepair. Some of the students attended school in Saybrook, some in Weathersfield, and others in New Haven. Jonathan's class began in New Haven but a few weeks later moved to Weathersfield. By 1719, the entire student body was once again assembled in New Haven, and the school was given the name of Yale College. Jonathan lived in a newly built hall and dormitory. The rent for his room was 20 shillings a year.

His studies at Yale consisted of Latin, Greek, Hebrew, geometry, rhetoric, logic, and the Bible. Jonathan, however, did not limit himself to these studies alone. Since the library at New Haven was the largest in Connecticut at that time, he took the opportunity to read a wide variety of different books.

During his second year at Yale, he read a book entitled *An Essay Concerning Human Understanding* by John Locke. The concepts in this book had a profound effect upon Jonathan Edwards. In later years, he described the pleasure of reading it as a "most greedy miser in gathering up handfuls of silver and gold from some new discovered treasure."

He also studied the works of Isaac Newton, who wrote that the universe operated according to well-structured laws, some of which could be figured mathematically. To Edwards, this meant that God was not a God of whims but a God of order. His new knowledge did not weaken his ideas of God but rather strengthened them.

During his time at Yale, Jonathan Edwards experienced a spiritual awakening. After this time, God became very real to him.

By the time Jonathan was in his third year, he had grown to be a gangly six feet tall and was rather quiet and withdrawn. He served as a college butler, a duty that meant he portioned out the food at mealtimes. While it was an honor to serve the other students, the job kept him from developing close friendships with the other students at Yale.

Something special occurred before the end of his second year. Jonathan experienced a **conversion,** a change in belief unlike anything that had happened to him before. Describing the experience in his *Personal Narrative,* he said he remembered the moment quite clearly.

He was reading his Bible and had come to 1 Timothy 1:7, which read: *Now unto the King eternal, immortal, invisible, the only wise God, be honor and glory for ever and ever, Amen.* As he read these words there came into his soul "a sense of the glory of the Divine Being." He thought, "How excellent a Being that was, and how happy I should be if I might enjoy that God . . . and be as it were swallowed up in him for ever." He then prayed to God that he might "enjoy him," and "in a manner quite different from what I used to do; with a new sort of affection."

After this time, God became very real to Jonathan and his dearest object of devotion. His spiritual conversion changed his entire life–even his dread fear of thunderstorms was gone.

Before, I used to be uncommonly terri-
fied with thunder . . . but now, on the
contrary, it rejoiced me. I felt God, so
to speak, at the first appearance of a
thunder storm; and used to take the
opportunity, at such times, . . . [to] see
the lightnings play, and hear the majes-
tic and awful voice of God's thunder.

After graduating from Yale in September
1720 at the head of his class, Jonathan remained
at the school for two more years. During this
time, he studied to prepare for the work of the
ministry. At the close of the two years, he passed
his prerequisite trials and was licensed to preach
the gospel.

Jonathan immediately received a number of
invitations from various churches. He answered
the call of a small Scotch Presbyterian church in
the growing city of New York. He moved there
in August 1722.

This church had broken off from the first Presbyterian church and met in a building on William
Street between Liberty and Wall Streets. He lived

While living in New York, Jonathan Edwards would often find peace and solitude walking along the banks of the Hudson River.

there with a man named John Smith and Smith's mother. The two men became close friends.

Because New York was still a small village in 1722, Jonathan often visited a solitary place away from town on the banks of the Hudson River. Sometimes Mr. Smith would come along and the two would walk together and talk about God.

While this was the first time the young preacher had been so far from home, he made no mention of homesickness in his diaries. In fact, the stay in New York seemed to have been a deeply spiritual experience. He spent much of his time reading his Bible and found new joy in the Scriptures.

> I had . . . greatest delight in the holy Scriptures, of any book whatsoever. Often-times in reading it, every word seemed to touch my heart . . . . [I] [u]sed often-times to dwell long on one sentence, to see the wonders contained in it; and yet almost every sentence seemed to be full of wonders.

By the next spring, he saw that the wages paid by the small church were not enough for him to make a living. He decided to return home, so he boarded a ship for Connecticut. Reluctantly he parted from Madam Smith and John. The summer of 1723 was spent at his father's home in East Windsor. There, his thoughts often turned to his friends back in New York.

In the fall of 1723, he received his degree of master of arts from Yale College. Again, a number of invitations came from several congregations to serve as their minister. One was from his former church in New York. He turned down all of these and instead accepted an appointment to be a teacher at Yale.

Since there was no appointed leader of the college at this time, Jonathan became both a teacher and head administrator. Students addressed him as "Sir Edwards." There were 40 students in his first year, and 60 in his second. He had the difficult job of handling all matters of discipline among all the students. The joy he had known and experienced in New York was replaced by weariness and feelings of depression.

The illness he suffered in 1725 may have accounted for a part of this weariness. He first grew ill in September of that year and attempted to travel home to Windsor. However, he became so sick along the way that he was forced to remain at North Village, Connecticut. He remained bedridden there for nearly four months. For the remainder of his life, he suffered from long illnesses nearly every year.

While serving as a minister and tutor at Yale, Jonathan formulated a number of resolutions for his life. As he wrote them in his diary, he noted the time and special occasion related to making them. When completed, they numbered 70. These resolutions had to do with Christian conduct and behavior, as the following examples show:

- Resolved, Never to do any thing, which I should be afraid to do, if it were the last hour of my life.
- Resolved, Never to do any thing out of revenge.
- Resolved, That I will live so as I shall wish I had done when I come to die.

This set of resolutions, along with the Bible, became his lifetime guide for living.

The trustees of Yale were satisfied with his work at the school. They gave him a raise in salary and invited him to stay on. But Jonathan's path was leading in a new direction.

While he was out in public, Jonathan would always be seen wearing his ministerial black robes. Though he was often viewed as austere and unapproachable, he would always be open to visitors and willing to provide advice and counsel when needed.

Pastor at Northampton

Since the work of being a tutor at Yale was so difficult, one might wonder why he chose that position over a number of other offers. The answer may have been due to a very special young lady who happened to live in New Haven.

Sarah Pierrepont was the daughter of Reverend James Pierrepont, the first minister of New Haven. Her father was said to have been one of the first people involved in the founding of Yale.

Her great-grandfather, Thomas Hooker, also a minister, led the migration to the Connecticut Valley and founded Hartford.

Jonathan's eyes had been on Sarah Pierrepont for several years. When he was 20, and she was just 13, he wrote about her on a blank page of a book he was reading. This sweet, loving description has become one of his most-read writings.

> They say there is a young lady [in New Haven] who is beloved of that Great Being, who made and rules the world . . . this Great Being . . . comes to her and fills her mind with exceeding sweet delight. . . . She is of wonderful sweetness, calmness and universal benevolence of mind. . . . She will sometimes go about from place to place, singing sweetly; and seems to be always full of joy.

Up until this time, Jonathan had no real reason to seriously court the young Sarah. However, early in 1727, he received an invitation from his maternal grandfather, the Reverend Solomon Stoddard. Stoddard invited Jonathan to come to Northampton, Massachusetts, and serve as the assistant pastor. After more than 50 years of service, the aged Stoddard knew he needed someone by his side.

Solomon Stoddard held enormous power in the area around Northampton and was sometimes referred to as "Pope" Stoddard. His influence was felt throughout the surrounding communities. Stoddard had changed the old Congregational requirements for church membership. Under his leadership, the need for a profession of faith was dropped. In addition, individuals who wished to be members of the church no longer had to prove that they had experienced a conversion to the Congregational faith. Instead, membership and the taking of communion were open to everyone not "openly scandalous."

Jonathan was invited to conduct a service in August 1726 and was found to be satisfactory. In November he was invited to take the position of assistant minister to Stoddard. His pay was set at £100. He was also given £300 to buy a homestead and 50 acres of pasture lots. He bought a lot on King Street where he lived as long as he stayed in Northampton. As the town was built along the Connecticut River, crops were grown and became the main source of income for the area. The river was also the highway to other towns in this central region of Massachusetts.

Although the problems with Indians had passed, the town of Northampton showed signs of the dangers of those days. The houses, numbering nearly 100, were clustered in a circle around the fortlike church on top of Meeting House Hill. Signs of the old trenches used for protection during the attacks were still visible.

On July 20, 1727, Jonathan Edwards married Sarah Pierrepont. He was 23; she was 17. Sarah quickly became an able partner in the ministry. Having grown up in a parsonage, she knew what was expected of a minister's wife.

The cheerfulness that Sarah reflected was a welcome addition to Jonathan's life. She also brought a good deal of social grace and strong female leadership. While her husband was shy and quiet, she was known for her charm and wit. Totally devoted to Jonathan, Sarah willingly carried the responsibilities of running the home while he spent long hours working in his study or taking solitary walks or horseback rides.

The preacher was known to carry a pen, ink, and bits of paper and pins when he went for his rides into the woods. He would tie his horse and then walk and think and pray—a habit obviously formed when he was a boy. When an idea came to him, he would scribble it on a bit of paper and then pin the paper to his coat. He would then return home with several reminders pinned to him, which, with Sarah's help, would carefully be unpinned in the correct order.

Jonathan ministered alongside his grandfather for only two years. In February 1729 Solomon Stoddard died, leaving full responsibility of the church to his grandson. The congregation liked both Jonathan and Sarah. When

Jonathan fell ill in 1729, they came together to build a barn for him to show their support.

When out in public, the young minister of Northampton always wore his ministerial black robe. He wore buckle shoes long after buckle shoes were no longer in style. He was tall, thin, serious, and quiet. While some saw him as unsociable, the reason for his silence lay in the fact that he always thought before he spoke. Therefore, he was a man of few words.

He never made it a habit to pay continual visits to his **parishioners.** This was partly because he did not feel he had a talent for being entertaining. But it was also because he felt it was his duty to study and pray. He did, however, visit all who were sick or in need of his help.

This did not mean he was unapproachable, for his study was always open to visitors. There, they were treated with kindness and compassion. His advice and counsel were sought after, not only by his own people but by those who lived many miles away.

Jonathan had a special interest in young people. Often he called young people and children to his own house where he would listen to them and pray with them. He enjoyed presenting written questions to them, requiring that they answer him in writing. The questions were designed to be suitable for each child's age and ability. He wrote 14 pages to one young lady named Deborah after she had asked him how to conduct herself in a Christian way.

In the pulpit, Jonathan Edwards spoke without wild gestures, and his voice was low and his face solemn. In the early years of his ministry, the subject of his sermons often dealt with God's love and the blessedness of a close relationship with a loving God.

The sermons were carefully written out and he carried the notes with him into the pulpit, which was then called the "desk." While preaching, he often added thoughts that had not occurred to him while writing and studying. Later in his ministry, he wished he'd taught himself not to rely on notes so much. As the years passed, he felt it would have been more effective to memorize sermons.

In the course of the Edwardses' marriage, 11 children were born to them: Sarah, Jerusha, Esther, Mary, Lucy, Timothy, Susannah, Eunice, Jonathan, Elizabeth, and Pierrepont. Every evening Jonathan spent an hour talking with his children before going back into his study to write. His letters and documents from this period reveal his tenderness toward the children, especially in purchasing little playthings and bits of lace and ribbons for them.

All of his children were closely supervised, and none were allowed to be out past nine in the evening. Even when visitors came to their home, the children were still required to keep their regular bedtime. When the girls were older and their suitors came to call, the young men were not allowed to intrude on the "proper hours of rest and sleep, or the religion and order of the family."

Large families like the Edwardses' were common during colonial times. As the children grew, they would provide extra sets of hands to assist in the family business, farming, or household duties.

The early years at Northampton were probably some of the best of Jonathan Edwards's life. He and his family were well respected, and, for the most part, life was quiet and uneventful. But that was about to change.

The Pilgrims who arrived in the New World in the 1600s were filled with the anticipation of religious freedom. As further generations arrived, however, the religious fervor was replaced by strong feelings of individualism.

4

The Great Awakening

When the Pilgrims and the **Puritans** first came to the New World in the mid-1600s, they were filled with religious excitement. However, with each succeeding generation, that fire began to dim and then to die out. The new people who arrived on the shores of New England cared little about serving God. At least not in the manner in which the Puritan leaders had served God.

Those who settled in the region found life hard. They fought against the forces of nature, the wilderness, and the Indians. Poverty, hardship, suffering, and disease caused many colonists to become callous and cynical. There arose a strong feeling of individualism, while brotherly kindness often fell by the wayside.

The scattered churches were supported by small congregations made up of families living miles apart. Roads were poor and at times impassable. Horses were the only means of transportation. To add to the problem, there was a shortage of trained ministers. Those who did preach were mostly uninspiring.

From time to time, there occurred what were called awakenings or **quickenings** when the people "awakened" to the things of God and the **salvation** of their souls. These times were few however. There had been only five quickenings in Northampton during the times of Solomon Stoddard–which had spanned over 50 years.

For the most part, religion had become formal and external. Congregations looked to their preachers to tell them how to live, rather than looking to their own consciences. There was, however, a growing change taking place in

In an awakening, members of the congregation would become more aware of God and the salvation of their souls. Quakers would often come to this type of revelation suddenly during a church service or meeting and would visibly tremble with emotion, which is why they were known as Quakers.

Gilbert Tennent was a gifted young Presbyterian minister. In 1728, he became ill and feared he would die. He was saddened that he'd done so little for God. He prayed, asking God to spare his life so he could promote the kingdom of God.

Tennent survived the illness and became one of the fiery preachers during the "Great Awakening" of the 1740s.

Tennent, it was said, preached as "a dying man to dying men." Boldly he warned men of the wrath of God. Even the Harvard College elite were shaken by his talk of a final judgment and an eternal hell. Listeners were forced to face the issue of either accepting or rejecting salvation through Christ Jesus.

Presbyterian churches in Pennsylvania and New Jersey. Here, through the preaching of Gilbert Tennent and his three brothers, people were becoming aware of their own sins and crying out to God for mercy and **redemption.**

Gilbert Tennent was strongly opposed by many in his congregation, mainly because he insisted that all ministers experience a personal spiritual conversion.

Meanwhile, in Massachusetts, Jonathan Edwards was becoming more and more widely known, appreciated, and respected as a minister. The First Church in Boston invited him to present the Thursday Public Lecture in 1731. Such an invitation was a great honor, especially since it occurred during Harvard's commencement week. Because he was a Yale graduate, the event was quite significant. His address, entitled "God Glorified in the Work of Redemption," stressed man's total dependence upon God.

Two years later, he preached the second part of the message, regarding the nature of God's grace. This would eventually become Jonathan Edwards's first published work. It was here that he explained the difference between having an opinion about God and having the actual sense of God's grace. He said it was like the difference between knowing that honey is sweet and actually tasting the honey.

Late in 1733, his preaching began to have a different effect on his listeners. The Northampton young people, especially, began practicing their faith more enthusiastically. The young people began holding prayer meetings at one another's homes every evening of the week. In the spring of 1734, two people in the town died suddenly and unexpectedly. Edwards used the deaths as an example as he preached about the importance of personal salvation.

From this point, Edwards preached a series of sermons on justification of salvation by faith. This strong message stated clearly that an individual's church membership and approval by the church community were not enough for the soul's salvation. As with Gilbert Tennent, many were angry with Edwards and his message. Among those who opposed him were Israel Williams, Edwards's wealthy cousin, and other influential members of the congregation.

Skeptics, however, could not stop the wave that had begun. **Revival** spread to South Hadley, Sunderland, Hatfield, West Springfield, Long Meadow, Enfield, and Westfield. Edwards wrote an account of the revival to his friend Reverend Benjamin Colman of Boston. The letter told of people whose lives were totally changed. People stopped their backbiting and gossiping, he wrote, and the taverns were emptied.

Reverend Colman sent Jonathan's letter to his friends in England. In 1737, it was published in London under the title, *A Faithful Narrative of the Surprising Work of God.* Within three short years, it went through three editions and 20 printings. This writing made Edwards famous all over New England and in England and Scotland as well.

During these years, a similar revival movement was sweeping throughout England. One of the more well-known ministers of that period was George Whitefield, who had preached in England to crowds of more than

The Great Awakening swept through the colonies between the 1730s and 1770s. Preachers emphasized personal salvation by trusting God with the heart.

The Great Awakening led to many things in America:

- It divided the Congregational and Presbyterian churches into those favoring revivals and those opposing revivals.
- It allowed for educational advancements.
- It renewed missionary work among the Indians and slaves.
- It drew the country together, paving the way for a united front during the Revolutionary War.

John Wesley, founder of the Methodist Church, was born in England in 1703.

While attending Oxford, John, his brother Charles, and George Whitefield joined a small group of students in regular prayertime and devotions. They sought a deeper, spiritual relationship with God.

John considered the whole world his "parish."

A special conversion experience in 1738 changed John's ministry. Because he now believed in a "heart conversion" for Christians, the established churches were closed to him.

Thereafter, he traveled throughout the British Isles and preached in the open air. Thousands repented and were converted.

20,000 people. When Whitefield arrived for a visit in America in the fall of 1740, newspapers heralded his coming. In Boston, he preached to 5,000 on Boston Common and to 8,000 in the surrounding meadows and fields. These open-air meetings helped fan the flames of the Great Awakening.

Whitefield, like Gilbert Tennent, did away with the more formal manner of preaching. The new-style preachers told stories, painted word pictures, waved their arms in dramatic gestures, and walked about as they preached. These men did not encourage emotional responses from the congregation, but emotional responses occurred anyway. There was shouting, shrieking, weeping, fainting, and sometimes dancing, as listeners grew excited about receiving God's forgiveness. Their noise often drowned out the voice of the preacher.

John Wesley was strong in his faith and would spend many hours in prayer and devotion to God.

Whitefield's visit brought him to Northampton, where he stayed with the Edwards family from Friday, October 17, until the next Monday evening. On Saturday, at Jonathan's request, Whitefield spoke to all of the Edwards children and prayed with each of them. During the four-day visit, he preached four times from Jonathan Edwards's pulpit. While many New England pulpits were closed to the British visitor, this one in Northampton was not.

Edwards was deeply moved upon hearing the younger man preach. Respect and admiration between the two was mutual. Writing about Jonathan Edwards, Whitefield said, "I think I have not seen his Fellow in all New England."

In addition to Whitefield, other preachers were traveling swiftly on horseback from place to place speaking before crowds of thousands. Gilbert Tennent traveled to Boston in 1740 and preached every day for three months—often three times a day. Edwards, too, preached as an evangelist from pulpits other than the one at his parish in Northampton.

The minister in Enfield, Massachusetts, invited Edwards to come and preach there because his congregation had remained untouched by the revival. It was there, on July 8, 1741, that Edwards preached the sermon for which he is best known, entitled "Sinners in the Hands of an Angry God." He was unable to finish the entire sermon because people began crying out asking how they could be saved.

The traveling preachers stirred up much opposition. Many established church people, both preachers and laypersons, disliked the show of emotions (which some called hysteria) and the free-style of preaching. They complained about other preachers invading their areas. Dignified worshippers were irritated because these **revivalists** did away with the traditions and rituals with which they were comfortable and familiar.

Deep divisions in the churches resulted from the Great Awakening. The Congregationalists split into two camps, New Light Congregationalists favored the revivals, and the Old Light Congregationalists opposed them. Likewise, the Presbyterians who favored the revivals were referred to as the New Side, and those who opposed, the Old Side. (Years later, in 1758, with Gilbert Tennent serving as the moderator, the divided Presbyterian churches were once more reunited.)

The revival fires of the Great Awakening spread throughout New England and as far south as Georgia. It has been estimated that the revival resulted in as many as 30,000 to 40,000 new converts. Aside from the inner church division, the revival brought together many Congregationalists and Presbyterians.

More importantly, the Great Awakening drew all the colonists together. This bonding paved the way for the national unity needed for the War for Independence, which was to come 30 years later.

Once the fervor had quieted down, Jonathan Edwards took a long, hard look at the revival and carefully studied its effects. The writing that resulted was entitled *Religious Affections*. There, he admitted that while some outward signs may have been in excess, he was convinced that most were true manifestations of the spirit of God. He insisted that preachers should not be blamed if their sermons bring about "outcries, faintings, and other bodily effects."

He reminded readers that the Scriptures speak much of what he called "affections." He listed them as "fear, hope, love, hatred, desire, joy, sorrow, gratitude, compassion and zeal." Religion, he explained, was not just for church time but for every day of a person's life. And rather than Christians conforming to rules from the outside, true religion flows from the inside out.

Edwards's calm, rational look at the revival was a great achievement. No other revivalist preacher attempted such an undertaking.

The revivals also contributed to a change of Edwards's thinking toward church membership. As mentioned previously, under his grandfather's leadership, church membership was open to all serious-minded people, whether or not they professed to be a Christian. Likewise, they were allowed to receive **communion.** Edwards was convinced this practice was wrong.

Difficult though it would be, he knew he would have to correct that wrong.

After his dismissal from his parish in Northhampton, Jonathan Edwards accepted a job as a minister in an Indian mission in Stockbridge, Massachusetts.

Dismissed!

In the churches of New England, pastors often brought the misdeeds of the members to the attention of the entire congregation. For more than 100 years, ministers were known to publicly rebuke those who were "caught" in sins such as drunkenness or gossiping.

In 1744, a few young boys in Northampton got hold of a book on **midwifery.** "Granny books," as they were called, were common in every town but were not considered proper for the eyes of children. These mischievous boys, however, passed the book around to many of their younger friends.

David Brainerd was born in 1718. He became a Christian while attending Yale. His conversion was one of excitement and zeal, which drove him to speak of God wherever he went. He set aside days for prayer and fasting and loved to be in the woods alone with God.

Brainerd set out to be a missionary to the Indians. He spent as much as 20 hours a week on horseback in order to reach the tribes.

Brainerd died of tuberculosis at the age of 29. He was betrothed to Jerusha, Jonathan Edwards's daughter. Jonathan became responsible for publishing Brainerd's diaries, which became an inspiration to missionaries for decades.

When Edwards got word of this, he addressed the entire congregation, publicly reading the names of all those accused and some not accused. Later, the children were brought into the parsonage for questioning. Eventually, three boys confessed to being the ones who started the mischief. Their confessions were read aloud in church. While the case seemed to be closed, the people of the community were not pleased with the way it had been handled. As a result, fewer people joined the church in the years following the incident.

During this same time, the British were once again

fighting the French and the Indians. Saratoga, New York, a town less than 100 miles from Northampton, had been attacked and burned. New watch houses were once again erected around the town of Northampton. Still, several residents were killed in surprise attacks. The war raged on from 1744 until 1748.

It was in the midst of these days that Jonathan Edwards made a difficult decision. He knew he would have to take a new stand regarding church membership. For several years after the Granny book incident, no one attempted to join the church, so his views were not contested. In December 1748, however, someone did join the church–a woman named Mary Hulbert.

Edwards asked that she make an open profession of faith. At the same time, he presented a formal statement to the church committee regarding his views on membership. These views were printed in Boston and distributed among the church leaders in Northampton.

Mary Hulbert was more than willing to abide by the minister's request but strong opposition rose up within the church. Several powerful and influential leaders disagreed with the new rules. They were ready to get rid of their pastor. They accused him of trying to override the practices that Stoddard had set in place.

The only person who might have sided with him and protected him, Colonel John Stoddard, had died in the summer of 1748. Jonathan Edwards clearly felt the hostility of those who were against him. "[L]et me do or say what I will," he wrote in his diary, "my words & actions are represented in dark colours."

Throughout the attacks against him, Edwards remained calm and continually attempted to soothe the people as well. In the spring of 1750, he presented several lectures in his own defense. These were attended mostly by people from out of the area; his own parishioners stayed away.

Eventually, a council of area ministers representing the Congregational Church was called

Jonathan Edwards would visit all who were sick or in need of his help. He would often have to travel long distances to rural areas of the parish. He was pastor in Northampton for over 23 years.

in to oversee the matter. They found the congregation in such a turmoil that they voted that the relationship between pastor and congregation be dissolved. On June 22, 1750, the church voted 230 to 23 to dismiss their minister. On July 2, Jonathan Edwards preached his farewell sermon to his church. He had served the people of Northampton for over 23 years.

What followed was an awkward period of time. Edwards had a large family and little income outside of his salary from the church. What would he do now? Those who had supported him through the upheaval invited him to remain in the town and begin another separate church and serve as the pastor. Although this would have been an easy way out, Edwards refused. He could see how that might divide the town more so than it already was. Throughout this tumultuous time, Jonathan Edwards continued to conduct himself with proper dignity and goodwill toward all.

Meanwhile, the Indian Mission at Stockbridge, a town 60 miles west of Northampton, was looking for a minister. Reverend John Sergeant of Boston, who served as the commissioner for Indian affairs, had died, leaving the position vacant. The position was offered to Jonathan Edwards, and he accepted. The family packed up all their belongings and moved to Stockbridge, a year after Edwards had been dismissed from Northampton. He was not completely unfamiliar with the region or the town, for he had preached there in 1734 when he and Colonel John Stoddard traveled to the area together. Perhaps the remoteness of the town appealed to him.

In the early 1700s, when the white settlers came into contact with the Housatonic tribe in western Massachusetts, they found the Indians to be gentle and friendly. The settlers purchased land from the Indians in 1724 and began laying out the town of Stockbridge, nestled in the Berkshire Hills along the Housatonic River. The tribe, later called the Stockbridge Indians, remained nearby.

Because the Housatonic chief, Koukapot, was inclined toward Christianity, a **missionary** was sent there by the London Society for Propagating the Gospel in Foreign Parts. John Sergeant, then a tutor at Yale, was more than willing to go.

Sergeant built a schoolhouse where he taught the Indian children to read and write. He not only ministered to the Stockbridge Indians but also invited other tribes in the vicinity to come as well.

At the time of Sergeant's death, he had baptized more than 180 Indians. When other areas of the colonies suffered from Indian wars, those in and around Stockbridge were kept safe from harm.

At the time of Jonathan Edwards's arrival, the Indians and the few white settlers who were living in Stockbridge had been without a pastor for two years. Edwards received a warm welcome.

Stockbridge must have reminded Jonathan Edwards of the area around East Windsor during the days of his youth. In this small village, his time was no longer taken up with many visitors as it was in Northampton. Area churches did not call for his oversight and direction, and he was not called to sit in on council meetings.

In quiet Stockbridge, he was able to spend more time in his study than ever before.

He purchased the house that John Sergeant had built. It stood near the center of the village, facing south, and had a commanding view of peaceful rolling meadows. Within the house, next to the chimney, was a small room about four feet by six feet with one window facing west. Here, it is said, Jonathan Edwards spent long hours writing.

Nowhere do we find evidence that Edwards suffered from wounded pride, or from bitterness about his change of circumstances. He settled in and devoted himself to the tasks at hand.

His work with the Indians was not the groundbreaking work that had faced John Sergeant. Because Edwards did not learn the language, he had to preach through the use of an interpreter. In spite of the language barrier, he gained the confidence of the Indians.

With regard to the mission itself, he proved to be a good executive and administrator. He wrote

In Neshaminy, Pennsylvania, William Tennent built a log school. There, he taught children from the community. The school became known as Log College.

He taught languages and mathematics but also the Bible, and he filled his students with a zeal for God. His son, Gilbert, became a well-known preacher during the Great Awakening.

Many of his other students also became preachers. They traveled through the country preaching in barns and private homes.

When a new college was begun—the College of New Jersey—several Log College graduates became trustees. The College of New Jersey was later known as Princeton University.

often to the London Society, suggesting ways to cut back on wasted money, to create a centralized effort, and to stop duplicating work. In these letters he sounded more like a businessman than a missionary. Because of this, he also won the confidence of the mission commissioners.

When war once again broke out with the Indians in 1754, a fort was built around the center part of the town where the Edwards family lived. Settlers from around the countryside came there for refuge. The Edwardses served hundreds of meals to these visiting refugees. During this time, the Stockbridge Indians remained neutral.

By now, the older Edwards daughters were married. Esther had married Aaron Burr, president of the College of New Jersey (which later became Princeton University). Esther came to Stockbridge for a visit in 1756, bringing her infant son, Aaron. This baby would grow up to become the vice president of the United States under Thomas Jefferson.

Jonathan Edwards's grandson, Aaron Burr, was vice president of the United States under Thomas Jefferson.

The six years at Stockbridge turned out to be a blessing. For it was here that Edwards's best theological writings were completed–the writings for which he would become famous in the decades and centuries to come.

Jonathan Edwards was appointed president of the College of New Jersey, now Princeton University, in 1758. Although he only served as president for a short time, he made a great impact on the students through his preaching and lectures.

College President

Some have called the years Jonathan Edwards spent in the quiet wilderness of the Berkshire Mountains his "intellectual harvest time." His first published work from this period, entitled *Misrepresentations Corrected and Truth Vindicated,* continued to clarify his position during the problems at Northampton. This work was published in 1752.

In 1760, Joseph Hawley, one of those who spearheaded the attack against Edwards in Northampton, wrote an extensive apology. This apology was then published in a weekly newspaper in Boston. He was clearly ashamed of all he had done. Some have said it is his reading of *Misrepresentations* that caused him to write the apology.

Edwards's second work, which became his most famous, *Freedom of Will,* was published in Boston in 1754. This work is considered by some to be the greatest philosophical **treatise** ever written by an American. The basic thought behind the writing is the fact that when God reveals himself to man, man is responsible and has power within himself to respond to God.

In *Original Sin,* a work published in 1758, Edwards points out that Adam's sin, the original sin outlined in the book of Genesis, is every man's sin. Thus, every man needs Jesus, the Savior who was given to us by a loving God.

In his work, *The Nature of True Virtue,* he lays a foundation to explain how all arts and sciences have their roots in God. This work and two others appear to have been the beginning of a larger more inclusive work that was never finished.

One can easily envision Jonathan Edwards taking long rides into the surrounding hills to think, contemplate, and pray. He then returned to work feverishly in his quiet study. He no doubt thought he would stay there and enjoy this quiet life to the end of his days, but change was once again on the horizon.

On September 27, 1757, Aaron Burr, Edwards's son-in-law died suddenly. Edwards was close friends with all the trustees of the college. In fact, he had been considered for the presidency in 1748, before Burr was elected. Shortly after Burr's death, the trustees met and voted to elect Jonathan Edwards as Burr's successor.

The invitation must have come as somewhat of a shock. Edwards penned a reply on October 19, outlining a number of reasons why he should not take the position. He cited his weariness and his physical ailments (one of which was "disagreeable dulness and stiffness"). He went on to explain that he was lacking in knowledge of higher math and of the Greek language.

His strongest objection was that he felt "swallowed up" in his study and writing. He had no desire to exchange this peaceful existence for the stress of running a college.

He closed the letter by explaining that he would neither accept nor reject the offer. Instead, he would seek counsel and advice. But he asked for one condition—*if* he accepted the position. He asked to be allowed to continue his studies while president.

Edwards then turned to friends in the ministry whom he knew he could trust. These friends met with him at Stockbridge on January 4, 1758. All of them agreed that while his objections were valid, he had a duty and a responsibility to accept the appointment. When they presented this decision, Edwards was moved to tears in front of them all. Such a display of emotion was highly uncommon for him.

It was decided that the family would remain in Stockbridge until spring. However, Edwards left immediately. He was accompanied by his daughter Lucy who was, as yet, still unmarried. And of course, Esther, the widow of Aaron Burr, was still in New Jersey as well. Edwards moved into the president's house to prepare it for his family.

Every Sunday, the new president preached to the students and faculty in the college hall. The student body, as well as the leadership, were pleased with his appointment.

He worked closely with the seniors during this time. He presented them with questions on the subject of divinity, providing them with an opportunity to study and write out the answers. Each student enjoyed the instruction he received from the president and his reactions to their answers.

Edwards expressed to his daughters that all his fears of taking the position had not come to pass. He now realized that he could devote himself fully to the work.

All through the spring, smallpox had spread throughout New England and scores of people had already died. In the 1700s, an **inoculation** against smallpox was available (which was different than a vaccination, later discovered by

Edward Jenner). An inoculation was a form of a disease injected into a patient in order to stimulate disease-fighting antibodies. While the inoculation could be hazardous, it was not nearly as deadly as the disease itself.

Jonathan Edwards had decided many years earlier that if the situation ever called for it, he would willingly receive an inoculation. The situation now seemed to call for it. He consulted the trustees and they agreed. On February 13, both he and his daughter Esther were inoculated at the same time.

He contracted smallpox "favorably" at first. This means he had only a light case. However, his age and poor health worked against him. Just as it seemed the danger had passed, a secondary fever set in.

When he knew he was dying, he called Lucy to his side and had her take down his last words. In the short discourse, he gave his love to his dear wife and children. He also requested that his funeral be simple, not elaborate.

Those who stood about ministering to him in the last days and hours were certain he had no capability to speak, hear, or understand. To their surprise, he began to speak a few words clearly: "Trust in God, and ye need not fear." These were his last words. Jonathan Edwards died on March 22, 1758.

In a letter to Edwards's widow, the attending physician wrote, "And never did any person expire with more perfect freedom of pain . . . but in the most proper sense of the words, he really fell asleep." A short two weeks later, Esther too had a flare-up from her inoculation. She followed her father in death.

The next fall, Sarah Edwards traveled to Philadelphia to fetch Esther's two small children. She died there in Philadelphia and was later buried at Princeton next to Jonathan, Esther, and her son-in-law, Aaron Burr.

While Jonathan Edwards was considered one of the greatest American thinkers, his own idea of himself was based on his deep belief in God.

Edwards did not simply tell his listeners and readers about empty religion; he showed them how to live a life in which God was very real and near.

As years have passed, most of the controversies surrounding Edwards's life have been forgotten. But the works and the life of Jonathan Edwards will be studied and appreciated for generations to come.

GLOSSARY

awakening a revival of religion

communion taking the sacraments (bread and wine) that represent the body and blood of Jesus

conversion a change in which a person adopts a new belief

inoculation the act of introducing a sickness to stimulate the production of antibodies

midwifery the practice of assisting in the delivery of a baby

missionary a person who is sent on a religious mission to convert nonbelievers

parishioner a member of a church or parish

parsonage the official dwelling for the parson or minister

Puritans a group of English Protestants in the 16th and 17th centuries who wished to simplify ceremonies and creeds of the Church of England

quickening the process of coming to life

redemption salvation from sin and its consequences

revival a meeting or series of meetings for the purpose of reawakening religious faith

revivalist a person who conducts religious revivals

salvation deliverance from destruction or from sin

theology the study of the nature of God and man's relationship to God

treatise a formal account in writing of some subject

vestibule a small entrance hall

CHRONOLOGY

1703 Jonathan Edwards is born October 5, in East Windsor, Connecticut.

1716–20 Attends Yale College.

1722–23 Becomes minister at a Scotch Presbyterian Church in New York City.

1724 Begins two-year tutorship at Yale.

1726 Becomes assistant minister in Northampton, Massachusetts, with his grandfather, Solomon Stoddard.

1727 Marries Sarah Pierrepont on July 20.

1729 Becomes full pastor upon the death of Solomon Stoddard.

1734 Revival breaks out in Northampton.

1737 Edwards defends the revival by writing *A Faithful Narrative of the Surprising Work of God*.

1740–41 The Great Awakening; George Whitefield visits New England; Edwards preaches "Sinners in the Hands of an Angry God."

1750 Edwards dismissed as pastor of church in Northampton.

1751 Becomes pastor and missionary to Indians in Stockbridge, Massachusetts; does his greatest writing there.

1758 Accepts presidency of the College of New Jersey (which later becomes Princeton University); dies from effects of a smallpox inoculation on March 22.

COLONIAL TIME LINE

1607 Jamestown, Virginia, is settled by the English.

1620 Pilgrims on the *Mayflower* land at Plymouth, Massachusetts.

1623 The Dutch settle New Netherlands, the colony that later becomes New York.

1630 Massachusetts Bay Colony is started.

1634 Maryland is settled as a Roman Catholic colony. Later Maryland becomes a safe place for people with different religious beliefs.

1636 Roger Williams is thrown out of the Massachusetts Bay Colony. He settles Rhode Island, the first colony to give people freedom of religion.

1682 William Penn forms the colony of Pennsylvania.

1688 Pennsylvania Quakers make the first formal protest against slavery.

1692 Trials for witchcraft are held in Salem, Massachusetts.

1712 Slaves revolt in New York. Twenty-one blacks are killed as punishment.

1720 Major smallpox outbreak occurs in Boston. Cotton Mather and some doctors try a new treatment. Many people think the new treatment shouldn't be used.

1754 French and Indian War begins. It ends nine years later.

1761 Benjamin Banneker builds a wooden clock that keeps precise time.

1765 Britain passes the Stamp Act. Violent protests break out in the colonies. The Stamp Act is ended the next year.

1775 The battles of Lexington and Concord begin the American Revolution.

1776 Declaration of Independence is signed.

FURTHER READING

Collier, Christopher, and James Lincoln Collier. *The French and Indian War.* New York: Benchmark Books, 1998.

Lutz, Norma Jean. *Maggie's Choice–Jonathan Edwards and the Great Awakening.* Philadelphia: Chelsea House Publishers, 1999.

McAulliffe, Emily. *Massachusetts Facts and Symbols.* New York: Grolier, 1998.

McNair, Sylvia, and Deborah Kent. *Connecticut.* Chicago: Children's Press, 1999.

Wellman, Sam. *John Wesley: Founder of the Methodist Church.* Philadelphia: Chelsea House Publishers, 1999.

INDEX

INDEX

PICTURE CREDITS

ABOUT THE AUTHOR

NORMA JEAN LUTZ, who lives in Tulsa, Oklahoma, has been writing professionally since 1977. She is the author of more than 250 short stories and articles as well as more than 40 books–fiction and nonfiction. Of all the writing she does, she most enjoys writing children's books.

Senior Consulting Editor **ARTHUR M. SCHLESINGER, JR.** is the leading American historian of our time. He won the Pulitzer Prize for his book *The Age of Jackson* (1945) and again for *A Thousand Days* (1965). This chronicle of the Kennedy Administration also won a National Book Award. He has written many other books including a multi-volume series, *The Age of Roosevelt.* Professor Schlesinger is the Albert Schweitzer Professor of the Humanities at the City University of New York, and has been involved in several other Chelsea House projects, including the REVOLUTIONARY WAR LEADERS biographies on the most prominent figures of early American history.